Native Americans

Ojibwe Indians

Suzanne Morgan Williams

Heinemann Library
Chicago, Illinois

Photo research by Amor Montes De Oca
Production by Que-Net Media
Printed and bound in the United States by Lake Book Manufacturing, Inc.

07 06 05 04
10 9 8 7 6 5 4 3

Library of Congress Cataloging-in-Publication Data
Williams, Suzanne, 1949-
  Ojibwe Indians / Suzanne Morgan Williams.
      v. cm. -- (Native Americans)
Includes bibliographical references and index.
Contents: Land of the Ojibwes -- A new world -- Living together on the land -- Ojibwe seasons -- Helper spirits and clans -- Birch bark homes and canoes -- Maple sugar and wild rice -- French traders and missionaries -- Dangerous changes -- Friends and enemies -- Treaties -- Government schools -- Life today -- Ojibwe spirit.
  ISBN 1-4034-0865-3 (lib. bdg.) -- ISBN 1-4034-4173-1 (pbk.)
  1. Ojibwa Indians--Juvenile literature. [1. Ojibwa Indians. 2. Indians of North America--Great Lakes.] I. Title. II. Native Americans (Heinemann Library (Firm))
  E99.C6W55 2003
  977.004'973--dc21

                          2003007474

Acknowledgments
The author and publisher are grateful to the following for permission to reproduce copyright material:
pp. 4, 5 Joseph Sohm/ChromoSohm Inc./Corbis; p. 6 Paul A. Souders/Corbis; p. 7 Annie Griffiths Belt/Corbis; p. 8 Roland W. Reed/Minnesota Historical Society; p. 9 Private Collection/The Bridgeman Art Library; pp. 10, 14, 17 Corbis; p.11 Ann & John Mahan; p. 12 Burstein Collection/Corbis; pp. 13, 30 Doranne Jacobson; pp. 15, 25, 26, 27 Minnesota Historical Society; p. 16 Patrick Robert DesJarlait/The Philbrook Museum of Art; p. 18 Frances Ann Hopkins/Canoes in a Fog, Lake Superior, 1869/Collection of Glenbow Museum, Calgary, Canada; p. 19 St Louis County Historical Society; p. 20 British Museum, London, UK/The Bridgeman Art Library; p. 21A The Philadelphia Print Shop Ltd.; p. 21B Heinemann Library; p. 22 Bettmann/Corbis; p. 23 William Armstrong/National Archives of Canada/Neg.#C-114501; p. 24 James Otto Lewis/Bibliotheque Nationale, Paris, France/The Bridgeman Art Library; p. 28 Phil Schermeister/Corbis; p.29 Bill Morgenstern/Earth Moods

Cover photograph by Minnesota Historical Society

Special thanks to Cheryl Geshick Gresczyk, Rick Gresczyk, Chuck Lilligren, and Lorraine White Crow for their help in the preparation of this book.

Every effort has been made to contact copyright holders of any material reproduced in this book. Any omissions will be rectified in subsequent printings if notice is given to the publisher.

Some words are shown in bold, **like this.** You can find out what they mean by looking in the glossary.

Contents

Land of the Ojibwes

Ojibwe people call Lake Superior *Gichi Gami,* which means "the Great Lake." They have lived along its shores for a long time. This area is in present-day Michigan, upper Wisconsin, Minnesota, and Ontario, Canada. Ojibwes remember that they used to live near an ocean that they called "The Great Waters in the East."

One story says that long ago Ojibwes moved. They traveled west along a river. The trip took many, many years. The Ojibwes lived at many places along the Great Lakes. Today, Ojibwe lands are in Michigan, Wisconsin, Minnesota, North Dakota, and Montana. Ojibwe lands are also in the Canadian provinces of Saskatchewan, Manitoba, Ontario, and Quebec.

The Ojibwe Name

Another name for the Ojibwes is *Chippewas*. *Chippewa* comes from the same word as *Ojibwe*. If you say *Ojibwe* fast, without the "O," it can sound like *Chippewa*. Years ago, people who spoke English wrote the word both ways. Ojibwes call themselves *Anishinaabe*. This word means "complete or original people."

A New World

There are many Ojibwe stories about Wenabozho, who was both an Ojibwe and a **spirit.** One story tells how he made the world. Once there was a great flood. Wenabozho climbed a pine tree to get above the water. The pine tree stretched taller and taller above the water. Finally, it could not stretch any more. Wenabozho was drowning.

Muskrats are small animals that usually live near rivers and lakes. Ojibwes say a muskrat helped create the world.

Another Ojibwe story says that Wenabozho also created the Apostle Islands in Lake Superior.

One by one, he asked animals to dive to the bottom and bring him some soil. But the water was too deep. The animals drowned. Then he asked a **muskrat** to get mud. The muskrat did it! But the muskrat died. Wenabozho blew the dirt across the water. The dirt created today's world. Wenabozho made land for the Ojibwe people.

Living Together on the Land

The land gave Ojibwe people the things they needed. They found food in the forests and lakes. They used bark from trees to make houses and **canoes.** Everyone worked together. They hunted moose, deer, **elk,** bears, beavers, and other small animals. They fished, grew crops, and gathered plants to eat.

Sometimes Ojibwes fished with spears. This photograph was taken around 1905.

Ojibwe girls and boys were taught to listen to their elders.

Children learned by helping adults with whatever needed to be done. They learned to listen carefully to older people. During the long, cold winters **elders** told stories. They told about the earth, the animals, and the **tribe.** Ojibwe people still make an offering of thanks before taking anything from the earth.

In Their Own Words

"I can remember my mother saying, 'Get up early and do your work. Do you hear me?' She told me to be kind to all, especially the old people."
—Nodinens, Little Wind,
    White Earth Ojibwe, 1915

Ojibwe Seasons

Life changed with the seasons. In very early spring, Ojibwes collected maple **sap**. In early summer, they peeled bark from **birch** trees to make houses, baskets, and **canoes**. Later, they picked berries. In places where it was warm enough, people grew corn, beans, squash, and pumpkins. In the fall, Ojibwes gathered wild rice. In winter, there was time to tell stories. Today, many Ojibwes still hunt, fish, and collect maple sap. They also gather wild rice, berries, and healing plants.

Ojibwes still use the bark from birch trees to make many useful things.

Each full moon marks the beginning of a new month for the Ojibwe people.

Ojibwe Months

Ojibwes name the months for each full moon. Different groups of Ojibwe people have different names for the moons. Many Ojibwes in Minnesota use these names for the months:

January	gichi-manidoo-giizis	Great **Spirit** Moon
February	namebini-giizis	Sucker Fish Moon
March	onaabani-giizis	Snow-crusted Moon
April	iskigamizige-giizis	Maple Sap Boiling Moon
May	zaagibagaa-giizis	Budding Moon
June	ode'imini-giizis	Strawberry Moon
July	aabita-niibino-giizis	Midsummer Moon
August	manoominike-giizis	Wild Rice Harvesting Moon
September	waatebagaa-giizis	Leaves Changing Color Moon
October	binaakwii-giizis	Falling Leaves Moon
November	gashkadino-giizis	Freezing Moon
December	manidoo-giizisoons	Little Spirit Moon

Helper Spirits and Clans

Many Ojibwes believe that the land, water, plants, and animals have **spirits.** The spirits, called *manidoog,* can be special helpers. The spirits may appear in dreams. Families prepare older children to dream of their own helper spirits. Spirits help people all of their lives.

This Ojibwe hand drum is painted with a bird design. Many Ojibwes believe that all animals have spirits.

Ojibwe children become part of their father's clan.

Clan Jobs

Ojibwes help their clans and **tribes** by sharing talents. Some history writers say that some clans had many well-known people with special talents. Here are a few:

Ojibwe Clan:	Special Talent:
Crane and Loon Clan	leaders
Fish Clan	teachers
Bear Clan	**protectors** or healers

Every Ojibwe belongs to a **clan.** A clan is like a big family. Clan members help each other. People from the same clan cannot marry each other. They are like brothers and sisters. Each clan is known by its animal spirit helper.

Birch Bark Homes and Canoes

The Ojibwes lived in small villages or camps. They built warm homes called wigwams. They made a frame of bent poles or sticks. They tied **woven** mats on the inside. They covered the frame with bark. They often used **birch** bark. When Ojibwe families moved, they rolled the bark coverings and carried them to their new camp. They used them to build wigwams there.

*To honor the **muskrat**, Ojibwes built homes that looked like muskrat dens. This photograph was taken around 1900.*

14

This picture of an Ojibwe man traveling in a canoe was made around 1885.

Ojibwes built strong, light **canoes** from birch bark. The Ojibwes used birch bark for many other things. They made things such as cooking pots and boxes with the bark. Little girls had their own small rolls of birch bark to play with.

Ojibwe Words

The English word "wigwam" comes from the Ojibwe word *wiigiwaam*. "Moose" in English comes from the Ojibwe word *mooz*. "Moccasin" comes from *makizin* in Ojibwe.

Maple Sugar and Wild Rice

In late winter, Ojibwe families moved to places where lots of maple trees grew. They called these places sugar bushes. There everyone helped collect maple **sap.** Sometimes Ojibwes drilled small holes into maple trees. Then they pounded hollow sticks into the holes. Maple sap dripped from these **taps.** They boiled the sap until it became maple syrup, candy, or sugar. Ojibwe families still enjoy meeting at these places.

It takes a lot of sap to make one gallon (four liters) of maple syrup. Ojibwe artist Patrick Des Jarlait made this painting.

Ojibwes call wild rice manoomin. *After they gather it, the rice is dried and* **roasted**. *Then it is danced on and fanned to get rid of the parts that are not good to eat. Finally it is cooked.*

Wild rice plants grow in **shallow** lakes and along rivers. In late summer, the rice seeds are heavy. Ojibwes bend the plants over the sides of their **canoes**. They gently knock the seeds out with sticks. Ojibwe people store the wild rice and eat it all year.

Maple Candy

Ojibwes make maple taffy. They also make solid sugar cakes. They used to make sugar cakes in **birch** bark cones. Today they use cupcake tins.

17

French Traders and Missionaries

The Ojibwes say they met fur traders from France as early as 1610. French **missionaries** wrote about meeting the Ojibwes in 1640. The missionaries wanted to tell Ojibwes about the **Christian religion.** Most Ojibwes were not interested in a new religion. But they were interested in trading.

French and mixed French–Indian traders were called voyageurs. They used canoes to carry furs to faraway trading centers.

*In the 1800s Ojibwe women made **traditional** clothes with traded cloth.*

The French traders wanted furs from beavers and other animals. They traded **kettles,** cloth, axes, and knives for the furs. Later, they traded guns. These things made work easier for the Ojibwes. The Ojibwes were good traders. They carried furs in **canoes** to trading posts in Canada and the United States.

Dangerous Changes

The Ojibwes had always known how to use plants to cure **diseases**. Medicine men and women treated sick people. But the Europeans who came to North America carried new diseases. Indians' bodies could not fight these diseases. Whole Ojibwe villages and families died. Many medicine men and women worked together to fight the diseases. Ojibwe healers still gather healing plants. Today's healers continue to cure diseases and help people feel healthy.

*Sometimes Ojibwe healers drew **symbols** on **birch** bark. The symbols helped them remember important ideas.*

This man is wearing a coin. Traders gave coins to Indians for furs. Each coin was worth one fur.

In the 1600s Indians trapped many beavers and other animals to trade with Europeans. It became harder to find the animals. Sometimes **tribes** had to move into each others' hunting grounds. Other tribes were forced to move west by European **settlers.** More Indians had to hunt for food in less space. Often, there was not enough food.

Friends and Enemies

European fur traders and **settlers** caused wars. They pushed Indian **tribes** onto each others' lands. Sometimes tribes fought each other for places to live and hunt. Groups of Europeans also fought each other for the furs. Each group wanted Indians to help them fight the other groups. The Ojibwes fought for the French.

The British and French fought for control of fur trapping areas. Many Indian tribes fought with one side or the other.

This was a dangerous time. Some tribes were killed, and others disappeared. For safety, the Ojibwes joined with other Indian nations. Together they won places to hunt, fish, trap, and gather rice. By the end of the 1700s, the Ojibwes lived across a very large area.

Traveling Together

The Ojibwes were once part of a larger nation with the Odaawaas and Potawatomis. Hundreds of years ago, they traveled together from the east. These Anishinaabe nations are still known as the Three Fires.

The Ojibwes, Odaawaas, and Potawatomis split near present-day Sault Sainte Marie, Michigan. Each group went a different direction. But they still feel closely related.

23

Treaties

Ojibwes wanted to keep their land. But in the 1800s, Americans and Canadians began moving onto Ojibwe lands. **Settlers** wanted Ojibwe lands for farming, mining, and logging. The governments of the United States and Canada signed **treaties** with many Ojibwe nations. Some Ojibwe nations agreed to let the United States and Canada use some land. The Ojibwes got money, **goods,** and promises.

In 1825 many Indian nations signed a treaty in present-day Wisconsin. They promised to stop fighting each other.

24

Settlers built lumber camps like this one on Ojibwe land.

These promises were often broken. The United States promised the Ojibwes that they could hunt, fish, and gather food on all of the land. The Ojibwes kept some land, called **reservations,** for themselves. But these reservations were too small to feed all the Ojibwe people. Some **dishonest** settlers cheated Ojibwes out of their homes. Later, the United States government gave away more reservation land to settlers.

Huge Area

At one time, Ojibwes controlled more land than any **tribe** north of Mexico.

25

Indian Schools

The Ojibwe people had lost land. But they had their way of life. Ojibwe children learned by watching, listening, and helping their families. They listened when their **elders** told stories. Then United States and Canadian government **agents** took Ojibwe children away from their families. They sent them to government or **religious** Indian schools far from home. The parents and grandparents of the Ojibwe children were very sad.

Indian students like these had to live far away from their families. They had to make many changes. Often they were lonely.

This photograph of Indian children and their teachers was taken around 1900. Life in these schools was very difficult.

The children were punished for speaking the Ojibwe language. They were taught that their way of life was wrong. They were made to feel bad about who they were. Government schools hurt many children. They kept children from learning Ojibwe ways. They changed the Ojibwe way of life.

In Their Own Words

"To learn anything well, do it with humor and fun. Take only the good of what you are learning. Use what you learn for good."

—Lorraine White Crow, Ojibwe, 2002

Life Today

Today there are at least 190,000 Ojibwes. Some live on **reservations.** Many live in cities and towns away from the reservations. Ojibwe people dress and live like their non-Indian neighbors. Most speak English. Ojibwe people work in all kinds of jobs. They might be doctors, pilots, or radio announcers. But often there are not enough jobs on the reservations.

Some Ojibwes still gather wild rice using **traditional** ways.

This Ojibwe man is a justice of the peace. He helps when there are arguments between people in his community.

Some reservations build **casinos** where Indian and non-Indian adults can **gamble.** The casinos bring jobs to the community. Indian nations spend money from the casinos on things such as schools, roads, and health care. Some nations use the money to **protect** or buy back land.

Reservations

There are Ojibwe reservations in Michigan, Wisconsin, Minnesota, North Dakota, and Montana. In Canada, Ojibwe reservations are in Ontario, Manitoba, Saskatchewan, and Alberta.

Ojibwe Spirit

Today, Ojibwes carry on their **traditions.** Many schools and community groups teach the Ojibwe language to children and their families. Some people meet to tell traditional stories in the winter. **Elders** pass on Ojibwe history. Many Ojibwe people work together to gather wild rice or make maple syrup, candy, and sugar. Healers meet for **ceremonies.** Some people are finding their **clans.** Some Ojibwe tribes are speaking out to keep the land clean and healthy. The Ojibwe **spirit** is growing.

This Ojibwe boy is ready to dance at a powwow.

Glossary

agent person who carries out government plans

birch tree with thin, smooth bark

canoe narrow boat pushed along with paddles

casino place where people gamble

ceremony event that celebrates a special occasion

Christian about a religion based on the teachings of Jesus

clan group of families that are related

disease sickness

dishonest not honest; someone you cannot trust

elder older person

elk large animal that looks like a deer but is much bigger

gamble bet money on a game or race

goods things such as food, tools, and clothing

kettle large pot

missionary person who teaches others about religion

muskrat small animal that lives along rivers and lakes

powwow Indian gathering or celebration

protect keep from harm or danger

religion system of spiritual beliefs and practices

reservation land kept by Indians when they signed treaties

roast cook over a fire

sap sugary liquid in a tree's trunk and branches

settler person who makes a home in a new place

shallow not deep

spirit invisible force or being with special power

symbol something that stands for something else

tap tool that makes a liquid flow, such as a faucet

tradition way people have been doing something for a long time

treaty agreement between governments or groups of people

tribe group of people who share language, customs, beliefs, and often government

weave lace together threads or other material

More Books to Read

DeAngelis, Therese. *The Ojibwa: Wild Rice Gatherers.* Minnetonka, Minn.: Bridgestone Books, 2003.

Lund, Bill. *The Ojibwa Indians.* Danbury, Conn.: Children's Press, 2000.

Todd, Anne M. *The Ojibwa: People of the Great Lakes.* Minnetonka, Minn.: Bridgestone Books, 2002.

Index

Nature Upclose

A Slug's Life

Written and Illustrated by John Himmelman

Children's Press®
A Division of Grolier Publishing
New York London Hong Kong Sydney
Danbury, Connecticut

For my friend, Frank Gallo,
who runs wild with the weasels.

Library of Congress Cataloging-in-Publication Data

Himmelman, John

A slug's life / John Himmelman
   p.   cm. — (Nature upclose)
Summary: Describes the daily activities and life cycle of a slug.
   ISBN 0-516-20822-5 (lib. bdg.)   0-516-26356-0 (pbk.)
   1. Slugs (Mollusks)—Juvenile literature.   [1. Slugs (Mollusks)]   I. Title. II. Series: Himmelman, John.
Nature Upclose
QL430.4.H55   1997
594'.3—dc21

                                                        97-29322
                                                        CIP
                                                        AC

Visit Children's Press on the Internet at:
http://publishing.grolier.com

© 1998 by Children's Press®, Inc.
All rights reserved. Published simultaneously in Canada.
Printed in the United States of America.
1 2 3 4 5 6 7 8 9 10 R 07 06 05 04 03 02 01 00 99 98

Slug
Limax

Slugs are closely related to snails. They both have shells, but a slug's shell is hidden under its skin. Land slugs live in moist places. They spend the day under stones and come out at night to feed. Slugs eat a variety of plants and mushrooms.

There is no such thing as a male slug or a female slug. Every slug is a *hermaphrodite* (her MA fro dyt)—sometimes it acts like a male and sometimes it acts like a female. All slugs can lay eggs.

As slugs move from place to place, they leave behind a slimy trail. The slime is similar to the mucus that runs down the back of your throat when you have a cold. The thick, slippery slime is produced by a gland in the slug's foot. The slime makes it easier for the slug to glide along the ground.

The next time you spot a slug's slime trail, see if you can follow it to the slug's hideout.

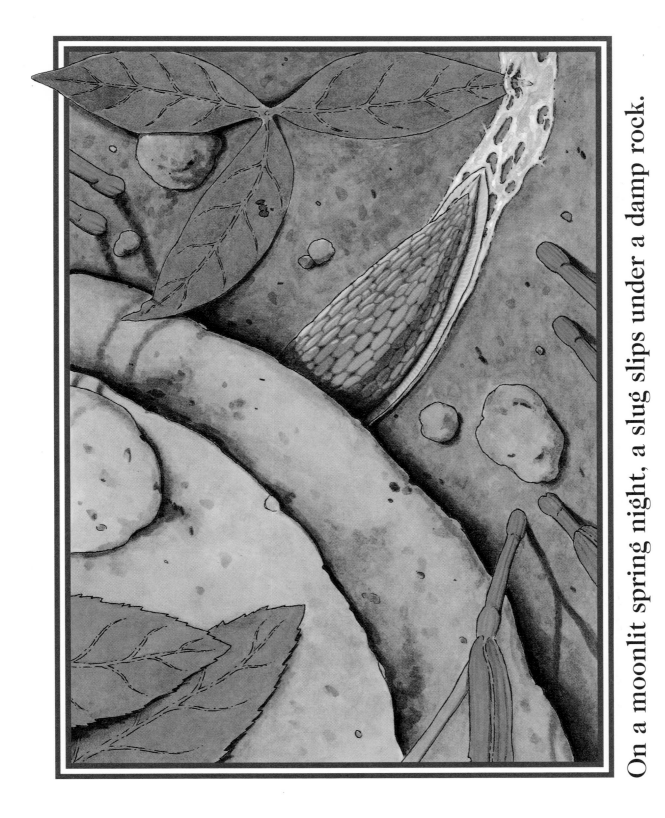

On a moonlit spring night, a slug slips under a damp rock.

The slug lays a *cluster* of eggs.

A young slug begins to grow inside each one.

After a few weeks, the first slug hatches.

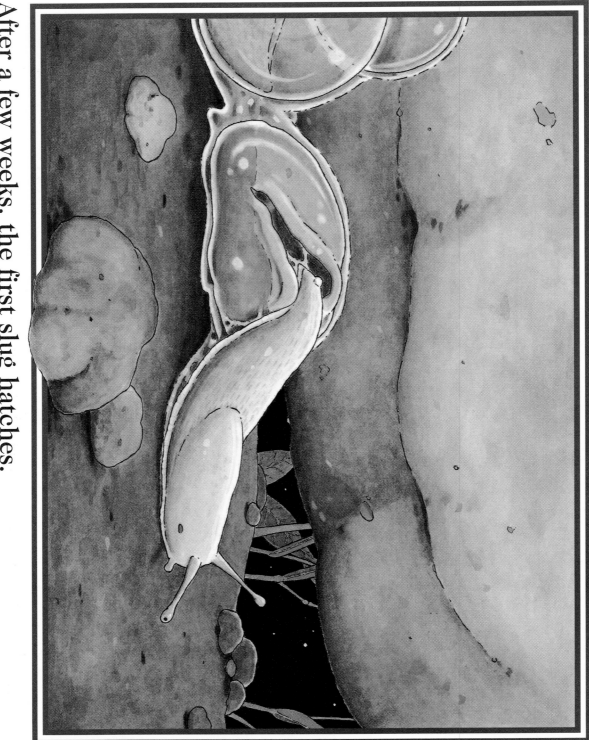

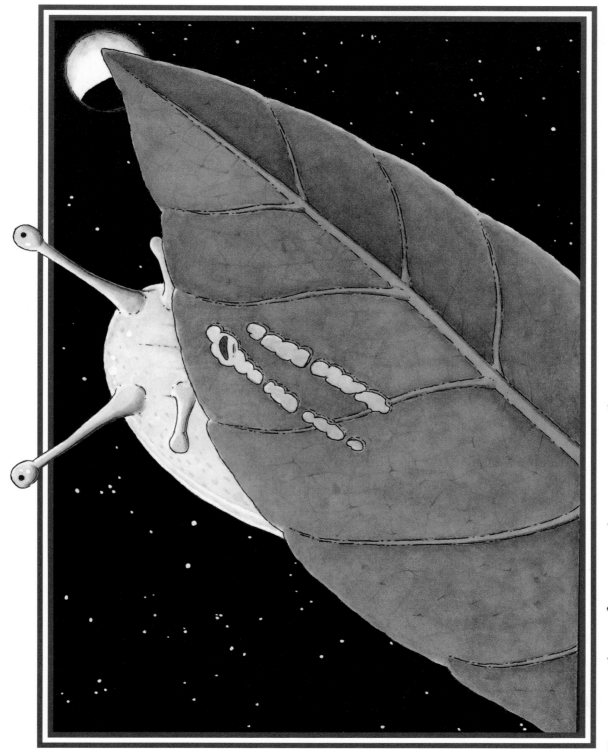

It searches for tender young leaves to eat.

By early summer, the slug has grown darker. It eats a *puffball mushroom*.

The slug spends its nights feasting in a vegetable garden.

One night, the slug smells something new.

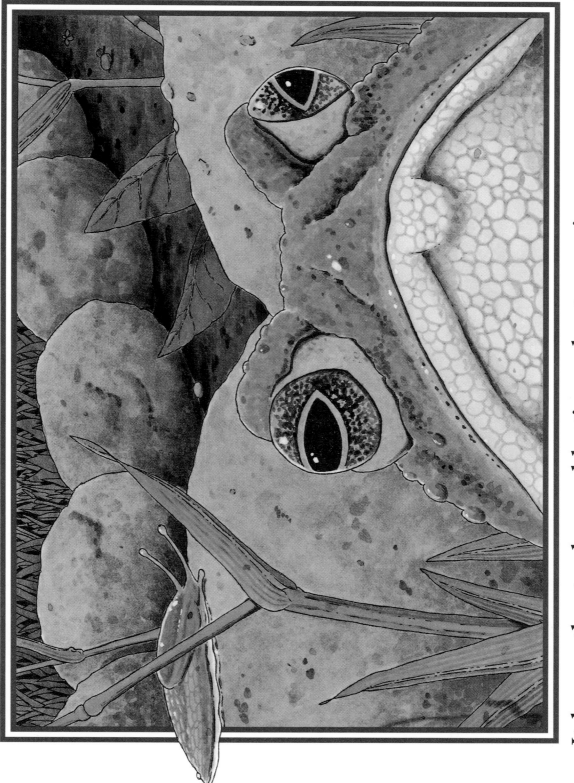

It leaves the garden and begins a dangerous journey.

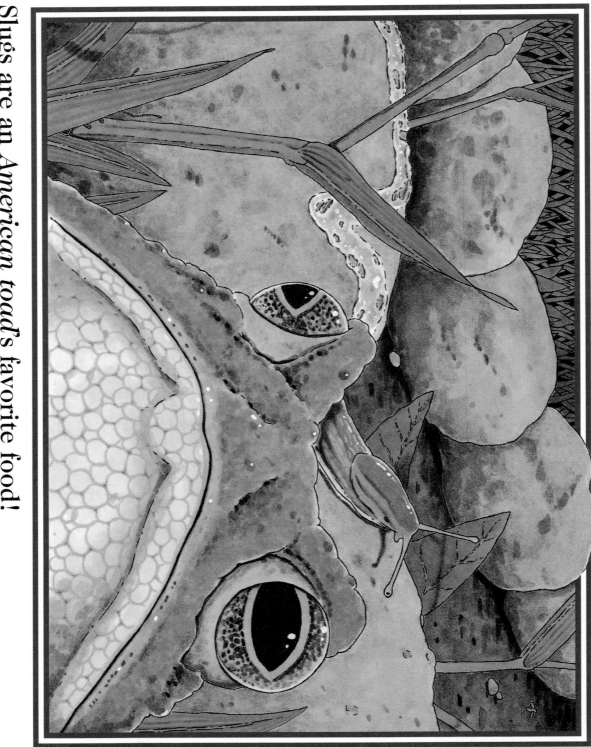

Slugs are an American toad's favorite food!

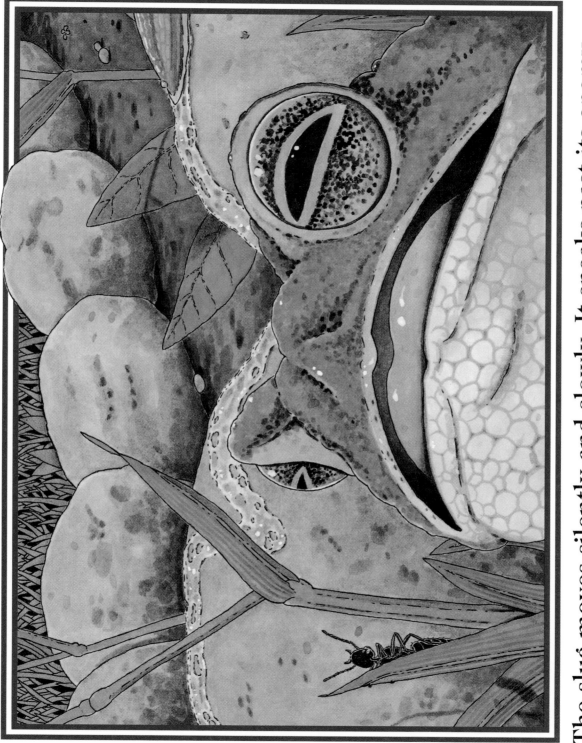

The slug moves silently and slowly. It sneaks past its enemy.

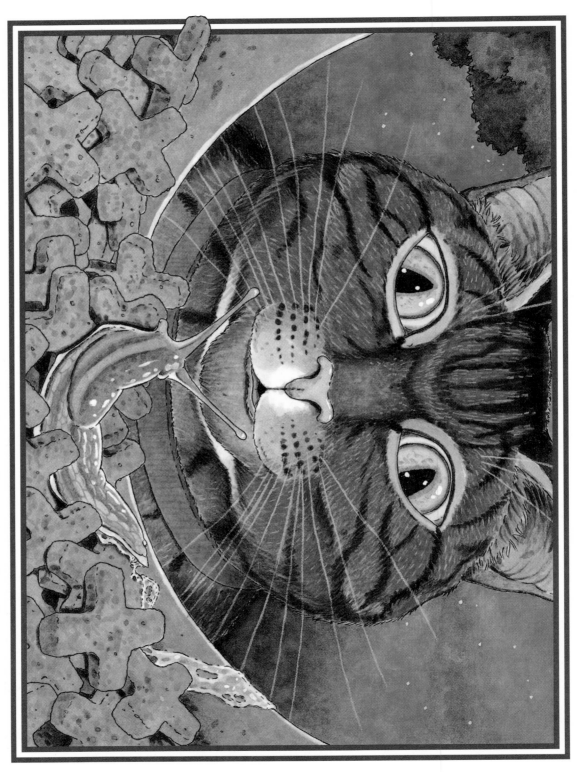

At last, the slug finds what it is looking for. Cat food makes a tasty meal!

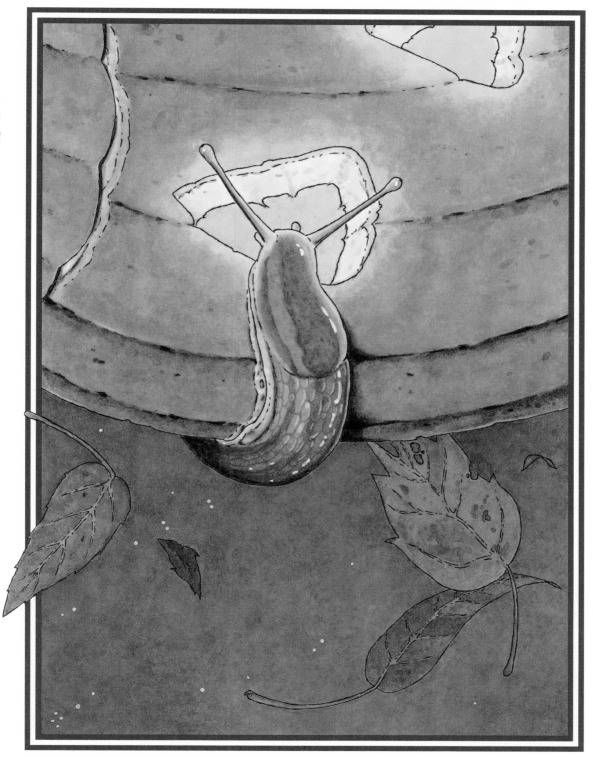

The slug is full grown by late autumn.

The slug does not like cold weather.

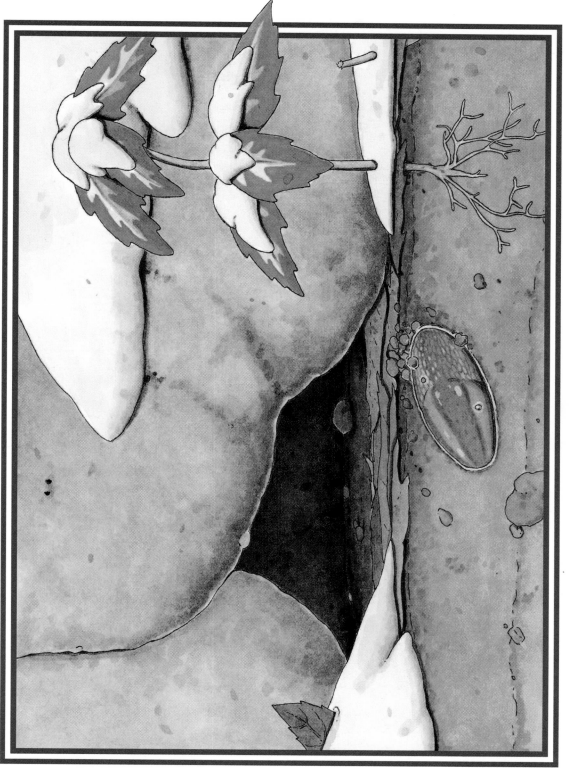

It spends the winter underground.

By spring, the slug is very thirsty. It soaks up water from a puddle.

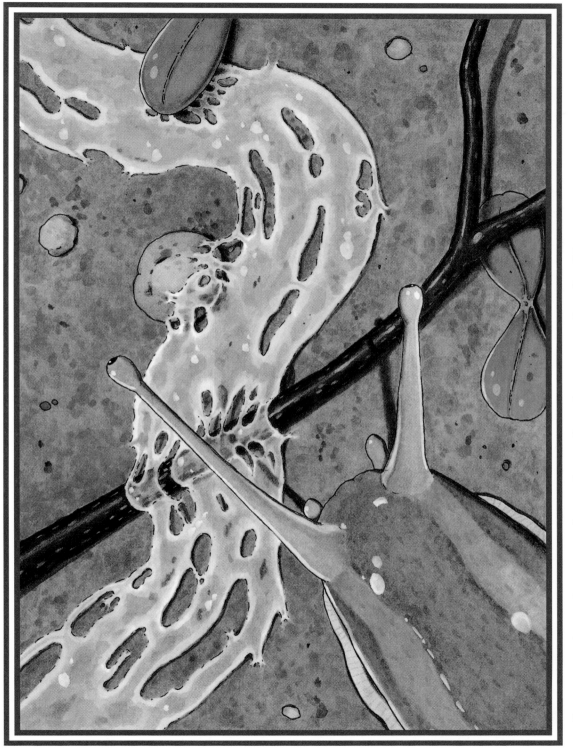

A few nights later, the slug finds a trail of *slime.*

The slug follows the trail . . .

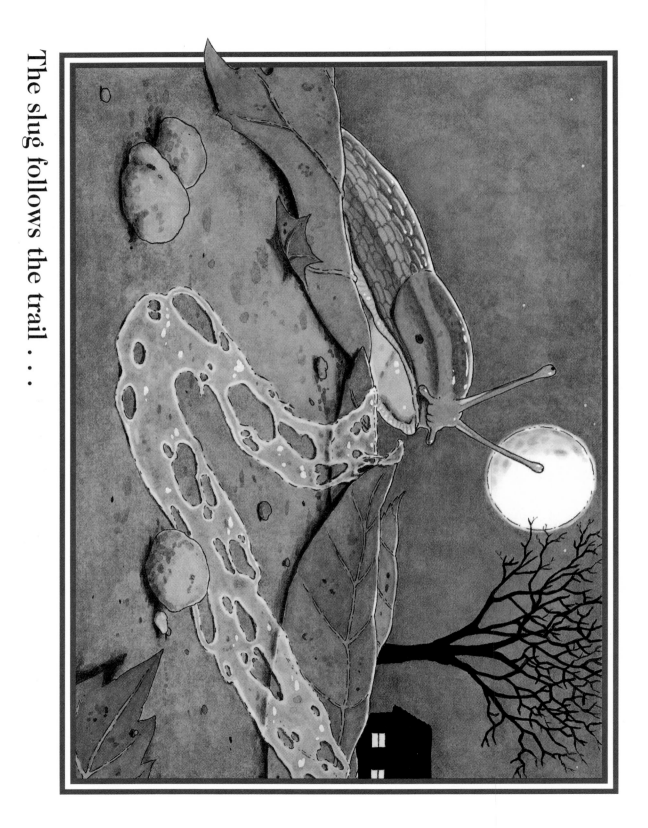

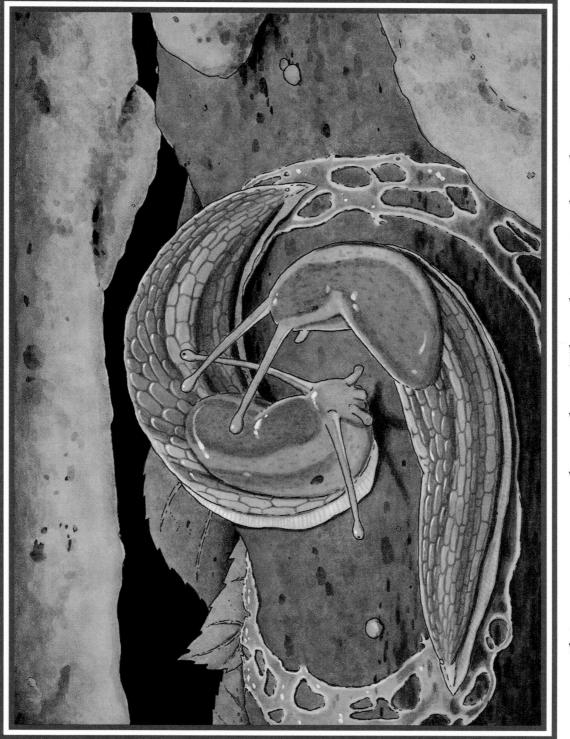

. . . until it meets another slug. The slugs circle, then mate.

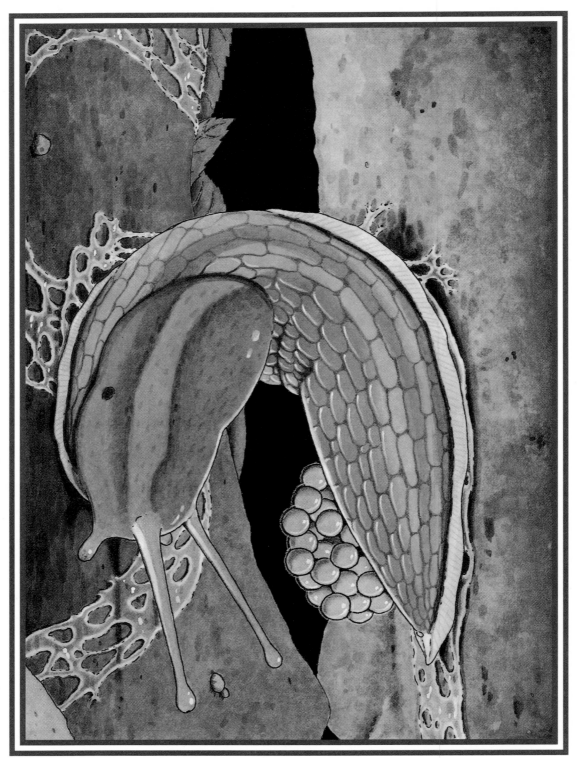

The slug lays its eggs on the bottom of a rock.

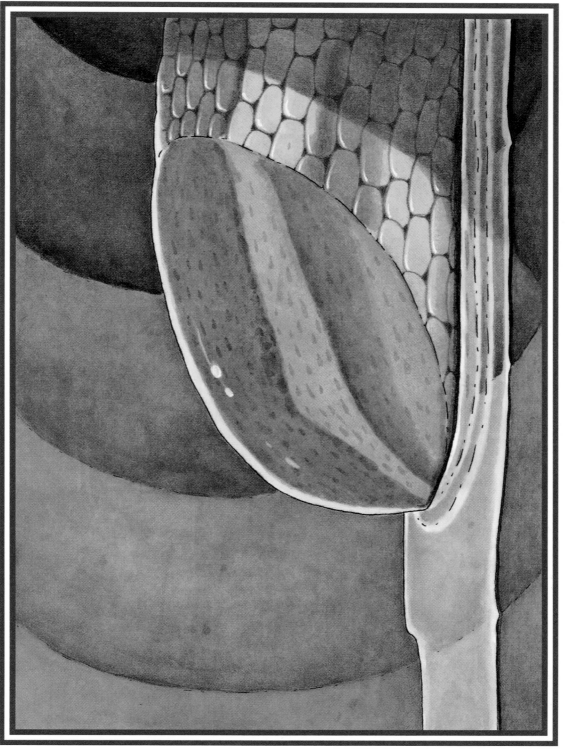

It finds a cool wet place to escape the sun's heat.

The slug's new home is lifted into the air.

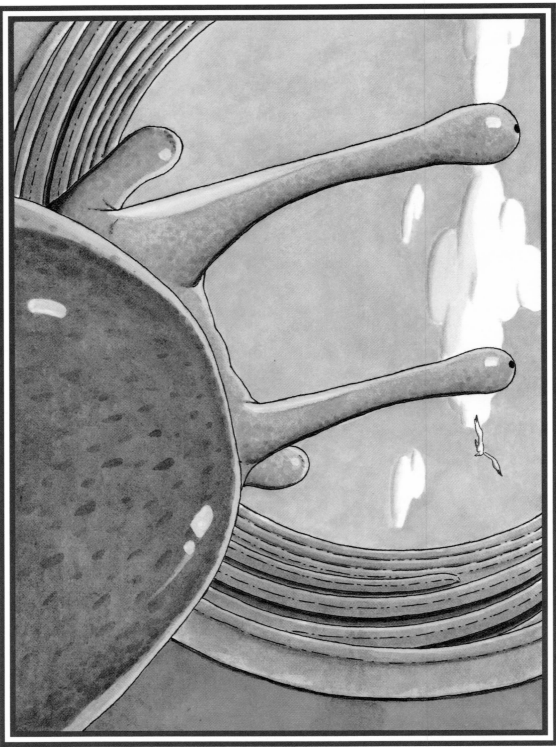

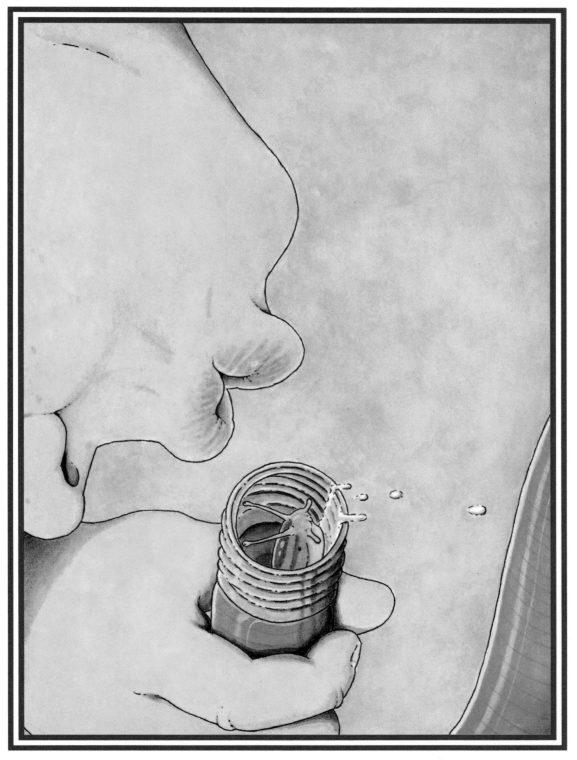

The slug senses danger, but there is no place to hide!

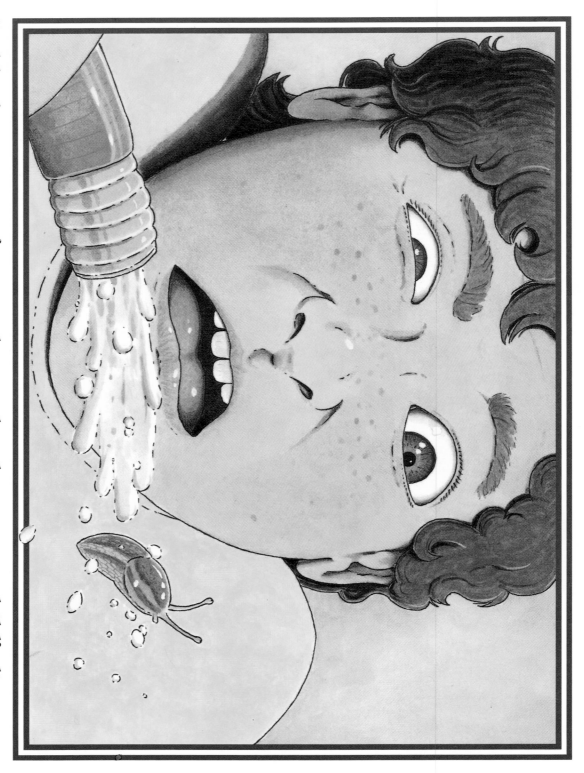

Suddenly, a river of water shoots the slug past a child's lips.

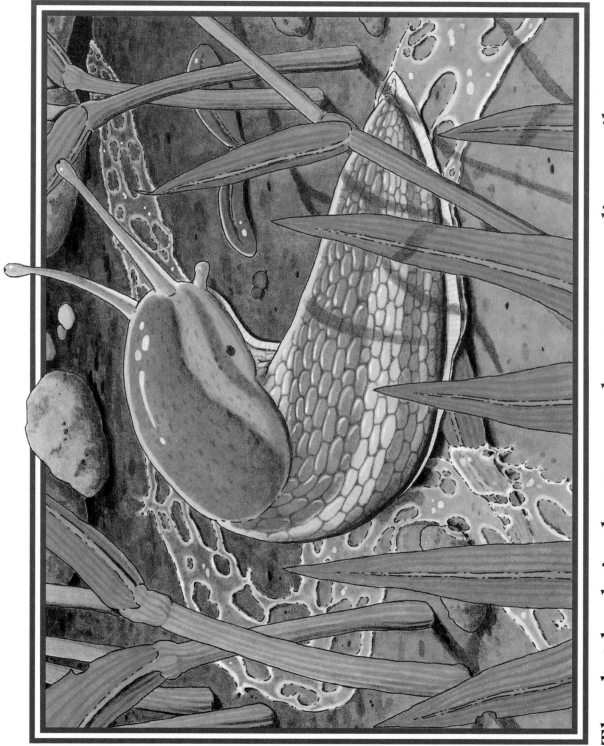

The slug lands in the grass and spots a new slime trail.

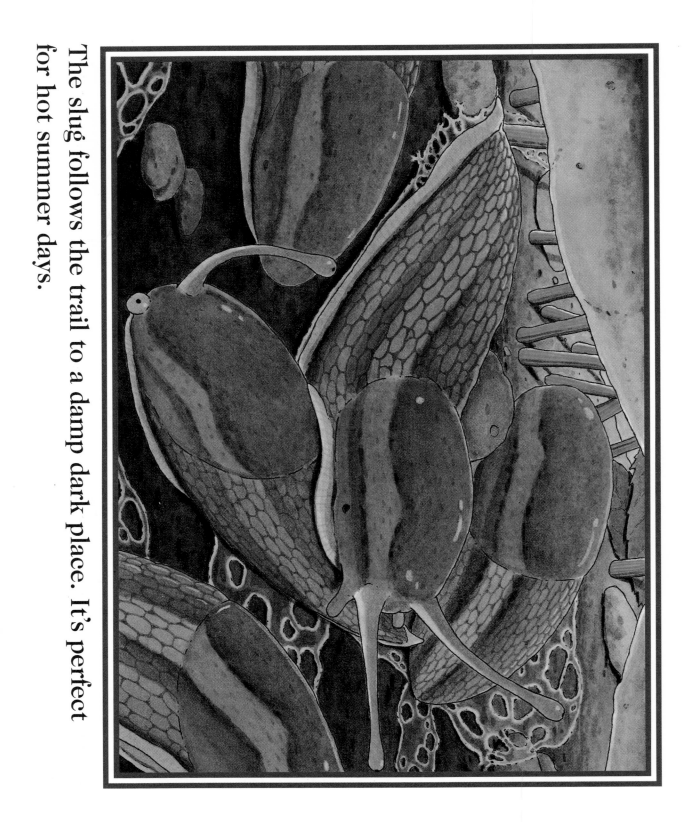

The slug follows the trail to a damp dark place. It's perfect for hot summer days.

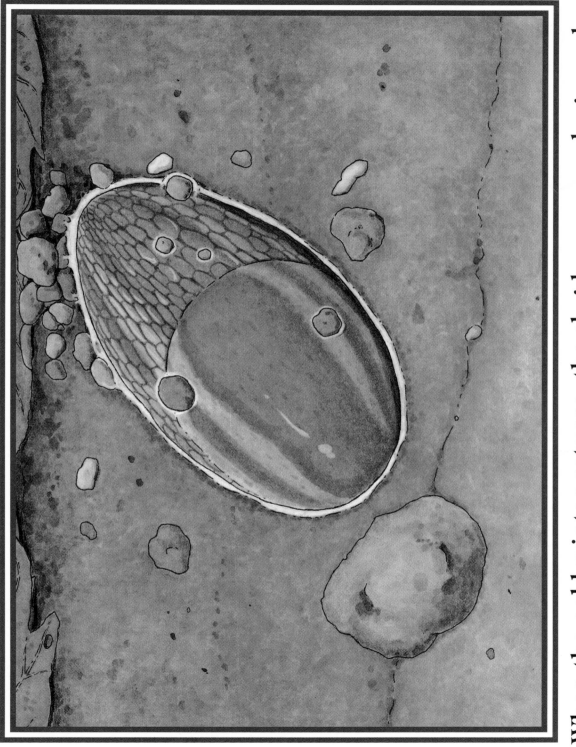

When the cold winter returns, the slug burrows underground.

And when spring arrives, the slug will have new adventures.

Words You Know

American toad—a toad found in most parts of the United States. All toads spend their lives on land.

cluster—a group of similar things found in one place.

egg—the hard protective layer that surrounds a developing creature. Young birds, frogs, insects, and slugs all hatch from eggs.

hermaphrodite—a creature that can act like either a male or a female.

slime—a thick, wet, slippery substance produced by a gland in a slug's foot.

puffball mushroom—the part of a fungus that drops spores. The spore of a mushroom is like the seed of a plant. A spore can grow into a new fungus.

About the Author

John Himmelman has written or illustrated more than forty books for children, including *Ibis: A True Whale Story*, *Wanted: Perfect Parents*, and *J.J. Versus the Babysitter*. His books have received honors such as Pick of the List, Book of the Month, JLG Selection, and the ABC Award. He is also a naturalist who enjoys turning over dead logs, crawling through grass, kneeling over puddles, and gazing at the sky. His greatest joy is sharing these experiences with others. John lives in Killingworth, Connecticut, with his wife Betsy who is an art teacher. They have two children, Jeff and Liz.